Justinian the Great: The Life and Legacy of the Byzantine Emperor

By Charles River Editors

Contemporary mosaic depicting Justinian I

About Charles River Editors

Charles River Editors provides superior editing and original writing services across the digital publishing industry, with the expertise to create digital content for publishers across a vast range of subject matter. In addition to providing original digital content for third party publishers, we also republish civilization's greatest literary works, bringing them to new generations of readers via ebooks.

Sign up here to receive updates about free books as we publish them, and visit Our Kindle Author Page to browse today's free promotions and our most recently published Kindle titles.

Introduction

Justinian the Great (circa 482-565)

The zenith of the Byzantine Empire was reached in the middle of the 6th century during the reign of the Emperor Justinian (527-565). The internal stabilization of the Byzantine state was completed, and Justinian then embarked on a wide range of external re-conquests. Justinian's prime directive was to restore the Roman Empire to its former glory in the west. He sought to strengthen the immutable law that Byzantium, the successor of Rome, maintained not only in the east but also the west, and by doing so, he hoped to revive the unity of the Roman world. In addition to attempting to conquer Italy and restore all the old dominions of the Roman Empire, Justinian also had to quell inner unrest by fighting barbarian usurpers, securing the borders, re-establishing religious orthodoxy, reorganizing the law, and reviving prosperity.

Accounts describe him as a stocky and ugly man, but he was deeply conscious of the prerogatives and duties of his position as a person exalted and close to God, and he was self-controlled in his personal life. From an administrative standpoint, he was an adroit diplomat and organizer who was gifted when it came to choosing collaborators and streamlining the administration of his empire. He was also married to Theodora, a woman of extraordinary beauty, courage, and intellect.

Justinian was profoundly religious, which ensured that he spent considerable time attempting to reestablish orthodoxy and guide the church into the future. Justinian even ensured religious uniformity as this was the same as domestic law. There was no real separation between the legal order and canon law.

At the same time, however, Justinian was a short-sighted emperor who was unable to come to grips with the fact that it was impossible to solve religious conflicts through wavering political compromises. He was also unable to stem the decline in the Byzantine economy and unwilling to form long-term plans for the future that would secure the northern and eastern borders of the empire against the Persians and Slavs. Naturally, since he remained so focused on the present, Justinian also engaged in grandiose propaganda schemes to promote his own glory, such as easy conquests, trading in luxury goods with far-away countries (including China, India, and Abyssinia), a well-planned publicity campaign carried out by his court historian Procopius and his court poet Paul the Silentiary, and a grandiose building campaign in the capital of Constantinople, which included the Hagia Sophia.

Ironically, Justinian's foreign policy is what he is best remembered for, despite the fact it was ultimately unsuccessful. Though he inevitably fell short of at least some of his aims, Justinian did make the Byzantine Empire a more efficient empire in many ways. The Nika revolt in 532 that precipitated the building of Hagia Sophia and the undertaking of Justinian's building campaign was the last major populist insurrection against autocratic rule, and the Marcellinus Conspiracy in 556 was the last of the aristocratic uprisings in the Empire. Justinian succeeded in setting up a nearly bribe-proof civil service, his bureaucrats created a well-disciplined army, and he also succeeded in giving the empire a uniform code of law. That code of law, the *corpus juris civilis*, or "body of civil law," remains the foundation of the legal system in many modern European countries.

Justinian the Great chronicles the life and legacy of the Byzantine Empire's most important leader. Along with pictures depicting important people, places, and events, you will learn about Justinian like never before, in no time at all.

Justinian the Great: The Life and Legacy of the Byzantine Emperor

About Charles River Editors

Introduction

    Chapter 1: Justinian the Person

    Chapter 2: Justinian Comes to Power

    Chapter 3: The Nika Riots and Hagia Sophia

    Chapter 4: Byzantine Feudalism

    Chapter 5: Justinian's Reform of the Administration

    Chapter 6: Justinian's Financial Policy

    Chapter 7: Justinian's Ecclesiastical Policy

    Chapter 8: Justinian's Foreign Policy

    Chapter 9: Justinian's Legal Reform

Conclusion

Bibliography

Chapter 1: Justinian the Person

Ruins of the ancient town of Tauresium, where Justinian was born

For hundreds of years, Justinian I has been considered the most famous and influential of the Byzantine emperors, even if he would've never called himself that. Traditionally, the line of Byzantine Emperors started with the Roman Emperor Constantine the Great, the first Christian emperor and the one who rebuilt the city of Byzantium as the imperial capital of Constantinople. Under his rule, the major characteristics of the Byzantine state emerged, and all Byzantine emperors considered themselves Roman Emperors. In fact, the term "Byzantine" was only coined by Western historians in the 16th century.

Justinian was born in Macedonia to the family of poor peasants from Illyria, or the present Balkans. Not too much is known about his early years, but as with all such figures, Justinian remains highly controversial to his contemporaries and descendants. His strength paved the way for becoming chief of the Imperial Guard, and his military valor helped him to climb the ladder of later military posts. Taking part in many campaigns, he won fame as a brave warrior, being able to please the influential nobles as well as the emperor. He thus reached a high rank as commander of the Imperial guard.

The historiographer Procopius of Caesarea in his official proceedings and in *The Secret History* has created a dual image of Justinian as a cruel and overbearing tyrant who was also a wise leader and tireless reformer. With its remarkable intelligence, willpower and excellent education, Justinian's extraordinary energy led to legal, administrative, and economic reforms that are all still part of the legal tradition of the West today.

One notable aspect of his reign was that Justinian was accessible to people of different ranks and was no respecter of persons. To some, this apparent accessibility was a mask concealing his ruthless, duplicitous and insidious nature. According to Procopius, his "calm and steady voice ordered to kill tens of thousands of any innocent people," but that could be said of many major leaders; Justinian was focused on the greatness of his imperial image and the mission of reviving the former might of the Roman Empire. Of course, there was nothing ordinary about those goals.

A strong influence on him was his wife Theodora, one of the most striking and original personalities on the Byzantine throne. Dancer and courtesan, Theodora, due to her rare beauty, intelligence and strong will, conquered Justinian, becoming his legal wife and empress. She had a remarkable political mind, delved into the affairs of the administration, and even received foreign ambassadors and diplomatic correspondence. In difficult moments, she showed rare courage and indomitable energy. Theodore loved power and demanded near-veneration on the throne. That said, there was nothing unusual about this, because humility was always seen as a sign of weakness, not mercy.

A mosaic depicting Theodora

When he became emperor at the age of 45, Justinian had experience in politics, and no one denied that he was anything but a man of mature mind and character, but given that he came from a peasant background, he remained in the eyes of the aristocrats a "yokel," even if they would not say so openly. He did live a relatively straightforward lifestyle; he ate and slept little, focusing entirely on the empire. He almost never left his palace and never left Constantinople. Despite all the luxury of his court, Justinian lived a very ascetic life, and the center of his life was theology. He would also micromanage affairs, personally relieving men of a bureaucratic post and confiscating personal property if corruption was uncovered. At the same time, he was a shrewd politician and tireless administrator who personally selected people of talent.

Even his opponents praised his generosity, mercy to enemies and care for the poor, but Justinian was always insecure and suspicious of anyone who became too powerful. He saw conspiracies everywhere, which, given imperial politics, was a realistic assessment of the situation. In a similar vein, he had a weakness for flattery (like many people).

Chapter 2: Justinian Comes to Power

His childless uncle Justin, after becoming emperor, immediately summoned his nephew to the capital, where he received an excellent education in the spirit of Greece. Thanks to his intelligence and energy, Justinian gained enormous influence over his uncle and began to actively intervene in all the affairs of state. In April 527, feeling the approach of death, Justin adopted his nephew as his co-regent, and when he died, Justinian became the ruler of the Byzantine state.

A coin depicting Justin I

The context of Justinian's taking the throne in 527 was not enviable. Michael Maas (2006) lays out the essential context as a set of social forces that any emperor had to face. First, Persian power was growing under the talented Khurso, which threatened Byzantium. On top of all that, less settled peoples such as the Huns, Avars, and even the Turks and Slavs presented problems and could be used by the Persians as an advance guard against the Greeks. Justinian bought off the Persians, the perennial enemies of the Greeks, so he could focus west, which arguably turned out to be a geopolitical mistake since it was impossible to keep the West under control. The best bet became the policy of the later emperors: developing a series of treaties and alliances that demanded the recognition of the Emperor as the supreme authority but did not require direct rule. At the very least, the main threat to the empire lay in the east, so the West should have been left to develop itself under the indirect rule of the Byzantines.

Of course, Justinian was so focused on the west because Roman authority had collapsed there about 50 years earlier, and the fall of the Western half of the empire meant that trade opportunities were lost, Roman cities fell into disrepair, and what was once a unified Western empire was now an unsettled patchwork of tribes and ethnicities. Justinian would spend a huge amount of manpower and money to reunify the two halves of Rome.

To the south, after the slow death of the Arian heresy, the Monophysite heresy, Arianism's opposite, took the loyalties of the Egyptians and Syrians. All of this played a huge role in Byzantine politics (Maas, 2006: 10-15).

Chapter 3: The Nika Riots and Hagia Sophia

Somewhat ironically, the building Justinian is most closely associated with came about in response to his first major crisis: the Nika riots in 532. A favorite spectacle for the inhabitants of Byzantium was horse racing at the circus, but the circus of Constantinople, as in Rome, was also the center of social and political struggles. It was one place where people of all ranks could be seen in the open, and in early 532, the circus parties (nicknamed the Blues and Greens), often at odds, united in protest against unbearable tax levies and started smashing everything in their path as they gradually approached the Imperial Palace. Justinian was desperate and ready to flee the city, but Theodora forced her husband to stay and fight, and eventually the uprising was submerged in blood by the local urban guard of elite troops under the command of the general Belisarius.

A contemporary mosaic believed to depict Belisarius

The social composition of the rebels was quite unusual. It was ruled over by the senatorial aristocracy and large landowners, but other factions were reflective of the interests of merchants and guildsmen. They were also divided religiously, as the Blues and Greens also represented Orthodox and Monophysite. Justinian was a "Blue," since it was the royalist and Orthodox party that had land and military power, while Greens were a moneyed class without either.

The revolt was quelled, but not before there had been considerable destruction of the city's monumental core. In the four days between the beginning and the end of the uprising - from January 14 to January 18 - fires started by the rioters burned out of control. The buildings destroyed included the old Hagia Sophia (completed in 360 and remodeled in 415 under

Theodosius II) and its neighbor Hagia Eirene, as well as the Augusteion, the Senate House, the Chalke Gate, the Baths of Zeuxippos, the great porticoes leading from the Severan core to the Forum of Constantine, and a large swath of buildings on either side of the Mese.

Excavated remains of Theodosius II's Hagia Sophia

Constantinople underwent one of its most important phases of urban development in response to the Nika riots. With so much of the capital's monumental core burned to the ground, Justinian undertook its restoration and rebuilding, and Procopius, the court historian of Justinian, wrote that the first project for reconstruction in the emperor's renewal of the capital was the new Hagia Sophia. He also lists other churches and then turns his attention to civic projects, which included the Great Palace and the Chalke Gate, the Augusteion and its Senta, the Baths of Zeuxippos, and the porticoes along the Mese. An enormous cistern, the Yerebatan Sarayi, was constructed under the Basilica.

Justinian's revitalization was spurred by the destruction that had taken place in the city, but he made it so comprehensive that it was necessary to extend all areas within the city's walls, as well as to the suburbs beyond them and the islands and territories up the Bosphorus. At the same time, while the project was obviously extensive and expensive, it did not transform the basic structure of the city because Justinian didn't establish any new civic projects like those that characterized the reigns of Constantine and Theodosius. The armature laid down by Constantine in the 320s and 330s remained the framework in which Justinian's project were constructed.

One major distinction that separated Justinian's projects from those of Constantine and Theodosius's campaigns, however, was the emphasis on religion. Much less civic construction was undertaken than was construction of religious institutions, which constituted a radical reversal from previous imperial urban renewal campaigns. Usually, efforts were directed at the development of civic spaces and institutions. In the city under Constantine, there were six religious foundations divided equally between pagan and Christian. By the time of Theodosius, it seems that the pagan churches had ceased to exist (probably due to suppression during the late-fourth-century purges of Hellenic cult), while the number of Christian churches had increased to 14. A century later, when Procopius was writing *The Buildings*, the number had already increased to 50. Thus, even though the urban form remained the same, the ethos had changed: Constantinople had changed from the embodiment of Roman ideals of civic splendor to a Christian city par excellence.

In his reconstruction efforts, Justinian employed an ambivalent approach to the Classical heritage of the city. In some places and buildings, Justinian placed old pagan statues from other parts of the city or from other places, such as Athens. However, as his reign progressed, he increasingly declined the use of public sculpture and the presence of antiquities, indicating that the antique world was no longer the cultural heart and soul of Constantinople, even if they had been under Constantine and Theodosius.

Hagia Sophia, the most lasting and tangible evidence of Justinian's reconstruction of Constantinople, offers information about what kind of images replaced antiquities. Hagia Sophia was built in the five years just after the destruction of the previous Hagia Sophia church on the same site during the Nika riots of 532. "Hagia Sophia" literally means that the church is dedicated to the Wisdom of Jesus Christ, and the church was the jewel of the city's redevelopment. Then and now, the church's complex dominated the city center, and its location on the brow of the first hill of the city means that it was visible to all those approaching by sea.

The monumental vaulted spaces sheathed in marble inside Hagia Sophia were intended to serve as a backdrop for imperial ceremony. It is reported that when Justinian stepped over the threshold of the new space on the day of its inauguration he cried out, "Solomon, I have outdone thee." Rather than referencing Troy, Greece, or Rome, the imagery of the church tapped into a new type of ancient history: the Bible. In her book *The Urban Image of Late Antique Constantinople*, Sarah Bassett wrote, "For the reference to Solomon was, of course, one that played on the dedication of the church, drawing the threads of Old and New Testament history - the wisdom of Solomon and the wisdom of Christ - into a definition of the Constantinopolitan present that saw the city less as the embodiment of the New Rome and more as the realization of the New Jerusalem."

In constructing the Hagia Sophia, Emperor Justinian set his sights on creating a church that would boast unheard-of size and lavishness. Marbles and columns were brought from all over the

Aegean and from as far as the Atlantic coast of France, all while the Byzantine emperor kept the marble workshops of the Proconnesian islands busy creating capitals, cornices, and plaques. Thousands of laborers were gathered from all over the known world to work on the building site, the brickyards, and the quarries.

Groundbreaking in so many ways, Hagia Sophia is also the building that established the modern concept of architecture. The profession of "architect" did not yet exist, as the empire had been dominated by Master Builders until that time, but Justinian did not think his Master Builders were up to the task of his masterpiece, even though they continued to be in charge of constructing many buildings in other parts of the empire. Thanks to the church's importance, the names of Hagia Sophia's architects, Anthemius of Tralles and Isidorus of Miletus, have survived, and historians know a bit about them. Both were mathematicians and scientists, and they were skilled in mechanics, geometry, and engineering, all of which were obviously crucial to the design and construction of Hagia Sophia. Anthemius was given the task of organization and logistics, which put him in charge of the vast budget of the project (the equivalent of a $1.1 billion today). That said, court historian Procopius wrote that the Hagia Sophia "has been wrought in this fashion by the Emperor Justinian...not by money alone that the Emperor built it, but with toil of the mind and the other qualities of the soul."

Not surprisingly, Hagia Sophia's complex structure created many structural problems, but Anthemius of Tralles and Isidorus of Miletus devised a remarkable plan in which the supports necessary for the large dome did not intrude on the cathedral's interior space, giving the impression that the dome floats effortlessly above the interior's massive volume of sacred air. Of course, the dome does not at all float effortlessly; though made of a relatively light brick and designed with vaults designed to minimize thrust and weight (and whose thinness is marvelous given the load they bear), the size of the building means there is an immense gravitational pull against it. The plan that mitigates this gravitational pull is remarkable but simple. A rectangle of 71x77 meters (230x250 feet) was laid out, and within that, a square was demarcated, inside which four huge piers (running north and south) were placed. The magnitude of the stone piers is more visible on the outside of the building than on the inside, while four arches swing across that interior space 70 feet off the ground. The arches to the east and west are free standing, and those to the north and south are embedded in the side walls of the nave and are hardly noticeable inside. These gallery vaults help buttress the piers. Four irregularly shaped pendentives link the arches, and from there the main dome rises.

The current dome, which has been in use since 1346, is a shell scalloped by 40 ribs and 40 curved webs. When the piers to the north and south rise above the roofs of the aisles to abut the lateral thrusts of the east and west archest, they indirectly also abut the lateral thrusts of the main dome. In conjunction with that, the 40 closely-spaced windows at the base of the dome are set between short rib buttresses that stabilize the junction between dome and pendentives. From those buttresses, the load is transferred downward to the four gigantic stone piers.

The fact that Hagia Sophia still stands after so many earthquakes and repairs might seem miraculous, but it is a testament to the work of its architects, and it demonstrates the importance of both science and math as critical aspects of architecture. Nonetheless, despite their calculations, in the end it turned out that Anthemius of Tralles and Isidorus of Miletus overstepped the bounds of design and the physical limitations of their materials. Hagia Sophia's first great dome collapsed in 558, after which it was reconstructed with a steeper pitch and ribbed construction in 563. This also brought with it other changes; since the dome base had been deformed by the base of the first dome, that caused the piers and buttresses to tip backward, the east and west arches to expand, and the lateral arches north and south to bend outward. The base was again regularized by broadening the arches to the right and left, and the large openings were replaced by seven small windows and one large upper window in the great tympanum. The gallery arcades and the wall they supported also had to be slightly shifted.

In *The History, V*, Agathias writes about the rebuilding of the Hagia Sophia from 558-562: "[Justinian] showed particular concern for the Great Church of God which he rebuilt in a conspicuous and admirable form from the very foundations after it had been burnt down by the populace, and endowed it with exceedingly great size, a majestic shape and an adornment of various quarried materials. He compacted it of baked brick and mortar, and in many places bound it together with iron, but made no use of wood so that the church should no longer prove combustible....Since Anthemius had long been dead, Isidore the Younger and the other engineers reviewed among themselves the former design and, by reference to what had remained, they judged the part that had fallen down, i.e. its nature and its faults."

Theophanes also wrote about the initial repair efforts: "On May 7th of this year, a Tuesday in the 5th hour, while the dome of the Great Church was being repaired-for it had been cracked by the preceding earthquakes-and while the Isaurians were at work, the eastern part of the vault of the holy sanctuary fell down and crushed the *ciborium*, the altar-table and the *ambo*. The engineers were censured because, avoiding the expense, they had not made the suspension [secure] from below, but had tunneled the piers upholding the dome, and for this reason they had not held. Having grasped this, the most-pious emperor erected new piers to receive the dome, and so the dome was built and raised by more than twenty feet in height as compared to the original structure."

Upon the second consecration of the church, on December 24, 562, Paulus Silentarius recited, "Now the wondrous curve of the half-sphere, although resting on powerful foundations, collapsed and threw down the entire precinct of the sacred house...Yet, the broad-breasted fane did not sink to the foundations,...but the curve of the eastern arch slipped off and a portion of the dome was mingled with the dust: part of it lay on the floor, and part - a wonder to behold - hung in mid-air as if unsupported..." He went on to describe how Justinian, while touring the damaged church, had praised the architect Anthemius, and how he reacted to the rebuilding of the church and its consecration. Finally, Paulus Silentarius praised the work, writing, "Thus, as you direct your gaze towards the eastern arches, you behold a never-ceasing wonder. And upon all of them, above this covering of many curves, there rises, as it were, another arch borne on air, spreading out it swelling fold, and it rises to the top, to that high rim upon whose back is planted the base of the divine dead-piece of the center of the church. Thus the deep-bosomed conch springs up into the air: at the summit it rises single, while underneath it rests on triplefolds; and through fivefold openings pierced in its back it provides sources of light, sheathed in thin glass, through which, brilliantly gleaming, enters rosy-ankled dawn..."

Arild Vågen's 2013 photo of the Hagia Sophia

The interior of the Hagia Sophia today

Chapter 4: Byzantine Feudalism

Restoring a centralized state in Byzantium was paramount in all respects, but of course, economic policy and landholding were the main sources of revenue. Slaves, serfs and tenants were legally defined classes, and, given the nature of the law in the East, the older patrimonial model of monarchy did not exist. Private property apart from the emperor was protected.

In Byzantium, slave and serf labor still functioned as a vestigial remnant of Old Rome. The use of slave gangs (often consisting of prisoners of war) intensified small-scale farming in the hinterlands, but since slaves work only to the extent necessary to avoid punishment, slave labor typically had poor standards, especially compared to serf labor.

The 6th century brought an increase in the rate of serfdom among the rural population. These were mostly from regions of barbaric groups having colonial status. As historian Peter Saris noted, "The late fifth century and, in particular, the reign of the Emperor Anastasius (r. 491–518) was clearly associated with a major consolidation of aristocratic power at the grassroots of early Byzantine society. Through the development of the offices of *pagarch* and *vindex*, magnate households tightened their control over the administrative and fiscal structures of provincial life." (Saris, 2006: 200). This was the reality that Justinian later saw as irrational, and from this, the 6th century drive to dispossess small landholders and even free peasant homesteads makes more sense. Draconian punishments were increasingly the norm for dispossessing elites of their lands too; according to the new legal code of Justinian, lands without heir, abandoned lands or lands confiscated from political opponents went to Justinian and the state. In practice, this meant that loyal landlords were favored and were, as a result, given a great degree of judicial freedom on the manor. Even the property rights of serfs were not decreed inviolable (as no property was ever inviolable in Byzantium); what truly mattered was the political stance of the lord.

A free "serf" in this context was a bit like a yeoman farmer. He was independent in the sense that he had a clear title of ownership, but other than that, the serf was essentially a renter with few rights. Slowly, this class became more dominant in Byzantium during and after the reign of Justinian, but the level of freedom it enjoyed was directly proportional to the strength of the emperor (Saris, 2006: 70-76).

While the era just prior to Justinian was a time of consolidation, this should not obscure the reality of many medium and small landlords throughout the empire. Growth was clearly visible in the major cities and the urban economy, which largely contributed to the resilience and stability of the Byzantine currency and basic confidence. The city housed the bulk of slaveholders and many of the slaves. Slave labor was used in certain crafts and municipal work (Saris, 2006: 125), and artisans and traders developed a guild system which was quite unlike the western variant. The guild was a taxpaying unit and was state controlled. It provided a certain minimum, especially a place in the relevant district of the city. Gold and silversmiths acted as a "central bank" in the early part of the 6th century, acting as loan-sharks and usurers.

Justinian's monstrous policy of construction is famed, but it required economic expansion that was only made possible by a strong state that could guarantee a certain level of security. Given Justinian's distrust of the manor system and elite landowners in general, to explicitly state that the government was the overseer of the "ascribed peasant" was a tremendous ideological statement. Saris explained, "Above all, governors were to ensure that landowners who erected signs over the estate settlements and urban factories of others, claiming ownership to them, were to have their own property seized. Provincials were to be banned from bearing arms or maintaining armed retainers. Lastly, Justinian ordered that governors refrain from issuing licenses of fiscal exemption. Under cover of these licenses, landowners had been collecting taxes from their peasants, only to hold on to them. The same illicit practice had also been engaged in, we should note, by the Church." (Saris, 210).

Thus, the economic system under Justinian seems to suggest a struggle between two contradictory tendencies of development. On the one hand, the ruling classes were rewarded for loyalty, and in many cases, the manor-system was permitted to function. There is no government that can dispense entirely with local elites, and the elites had every possible interest in dispossessing tenants and small yeomen. On the other hand, the new legal system steadily increased real economic links between the peasant community and the state, even at the local level, which solidified their property rights and maintained an economy which was largely independent and hence non-feudal. Indeed, the peasant community ultimately became one of the major tax-paying classes. They were responsible for paying state taxes and performing a variety of public works, including the construction of fortifications, roads, bridges, dams, canals and irrigation facilities. Needless to say, Justinian or any emperor with sufficient independence had no interest in dispossessing or alienating these classes.

Under Justinian, it was mostly landowners themselves who collected taxes from the peasantry of all sorts. Jews and other "foreigners" were used to "farm" taxes and, as is often the case, pocket any excess above their quota. When the emperor was weaker and the state seemed less focused, landlords and their allies ravaged the countryside. Proving the necessity of a strong central power, landlords, Jews, Armenians and Arabs took advantage of their status to steal as much as possible from the peasantry, who then could not perform the duties these same elites required. Justinian eventually created his own administration to deal with tax collection and ensure the local strongmen were not holding out.

The normal rate of interest that Justinian struggled to enforce was about 5% yearly, which was a deliberate reduction from the pre-Justiniac rate of almost 20%. When considering the previous aristocratic centralization, interest must be seen as the prime variable; high rates of interest without limits on arrears or collateral can make even a small margin of inequality become a pure oligarchy very rapidly. Fighting this destructive policy should be viewed as a major moral triumph for Justinian (Hudson, 2000: 135). Justinian sought to protect smallholders throughout the empire, but especially in Thrace and Illyricum against loan-sharks either in cash or in kind. Money loans were strictly limited to 5%, but in-kind loans were set at a maximum of 12%. Payments required the swift restoration of any and all collateral. Most importantly, Roman law in general and Justinian's reform in particular limited the accumulation of interest to no more than the initial principle (Hudson, 2000: 155-158).

When cash was used, any similarity to European feudalism ceased to exist. They became rate paying tenants and were obligated both by contract and custom. Needless to say, lords always aimed to increase the dues, but under Justinian's New Code, he ensured that even the poorest serf had the right to sue his lord in court. Then as now, the chances of victory leaned towards the lord, but in the case of a strong bishop or monastic presence, the peasantry often had a much stronger voice (Cameron, 2000: 336-340).

With the revenue generation in place as a result of those relations, the internal policy of Justinian was to strengthen the centralization of the state and strengthen the economy of the empire. In pursuit of this, he sought to enhance trade and the search for new trade routes. Constantinople at that time was the center of global trade, and throughout the rich cities of the empire, the rise of craft production and improved construction equipment increased growth consistently. This made it possible for Justinian to erect urban palaces, temples and fortifications in the border areas. Thus, while the Western Empire, torn to pieces by Germanic conquerors, became a conglomerate of barbarian kingdoms, Byzantium gradually entered a period of economic and political stabilization. The waves of barbarian conquests skipped over Byzantium to drain the West.

The economic recovery that started under Emperor Anastasius was largely prepared by the extraordinary qualitative increase of internal and external power of Justinian's era. Looking to major economic powers such as Thessalonika and raising the efficiency of tax collection gave the state the cash needed to finance all reform. At first, Justinian tried to unite with the Senators, but he soon realized that it was useless, and it is not an exaggeration to say that the Legal Code and his basic reforms aimed to crush the power of the Senatorial class. Although Justinian later engaged in a rapprochement with the aristocracy, he always understood the need to undermine its economic power. *The Secret History* of Procopius speaks of the confiscation of land of his opponents, and that those opponents were some of the most powerful men in the empire.

The attack on senatorial land tenure was one of the important tasks of Justinian's economic reform. The aristocracy, loathe to give up any power or money, hated a strong crown, and like nobles across Europe, they cared little for the overall health of the empire and would damage its interior strength if it meant even a small gain. In a sense, Justinian was fighting the development of regional "states" within the empire.

Another constant is that middle landowners normally loathe, resent and envy the very rich. Thus, monarchies from Peking to London have hired the services of this middle landowner class against the arrogantly wealthy. Significantly, these are the backbone of any empire, and the middle lords become the mainstay of the state, the administration and the army. Justinian's agrarian policy was motivated by the desire to attract these broad strata of landowners, so he began the process of ending slavery and assisting the middle lords in achieving better yields by changing agricultural methods. The transition to a more progressive method of farming was the urgent need of the time, and Justinian was able to direct and use this trend in favor of his reign. His approach favored the development of the "yeoman" landowner who was independent, patriotic and civic minded.

During wartime, the open fields were usually burned as their inhabitants fled for protection behind city walls, so drastic measures were taken to attract landlords to abandoned land and to the cultivation of wastelands. Thus, the legislation of Justinian established strong legal protections for the long-term lease; the basic requirements were the payment of a tax and, in return, the owner was given wide latitude in the use of the land. It created new incentives for improvements in agriculture and disincentives for the slave system.

Incidentally, Justinian offered long term leases to those who would release slaves from the larger estates in order to develop new methods of farming. Therefore, the lease system created a loyal class of middle-landlords who had taxes lowered and a grant of certain immunities for the sake of rapid repopulation. This included merchants in the cities, middle-class peasants, former soldiers, former slaves and formerly dispossessed landlords. The best part of the success here was that it helped anchor a new class of yeoman soldiers and citizens.

The tendencies toward oligarchy also explained Justinian's desire to eliminate all corruption both in the city and the countryside. Patronage, nepotism and even private prisons were signs of elite rule and their confidence against the state. The large landowner had his own militia, prison system, and even courts. Bureaucracy, for all its faults, was critical for the rule of law, or the elite would otherwise use their resources to dominate the countryside, reducing all they could to slavery. Without a bureaucracy, the elite patronage networks were all that could exist (Saris, 2006: 205-210).

Naturally, Justinian required his newly enfranchised lords in the middle class to give unconditional support to his plans of conquest in the West. He hoped that these circles could be easily tempted by the idea of a victorious reconquest from the barbarians, and he was not mistaken, but their interest was always short term. Old Roman patriotism still functioned, but the people also hoped to get a fraction of the spoils from the conquered provinces. The plans of conquest found a broad response, but when the war demanded exorbitant material hardships and too many victims, people began to waver (Rosen, 2007: 135ff).

Chapter 5: Justinian's Reform of the Administration

While Justinian wrangled with social classes, he also reformed the bureaucracy to stabilize the Byzantine economy. Aspiring to greater centralization and to strengthen its social base, the Byzantine government began a thorough reform of the state apparatus. Medium and small landowners, clergy, merchants, artisans, villagers and townspeople all suffered from the oppression of the elite-controlled civil-service, and hence, the streamlining of the administration and limiting the arbitrariness and corruption of officials became the foundation for all the rest.

To tackle the issue from the start, the sale of government posts was banned. This had initially been a desperate way to gain revenue, but it had led to government becoming the object of the highest bidder, so those who were wealthy enough could buy power that an ordinary Roman citizen could not. Of course, the price was steep, so the temptation was for the buyer to go back to his home district and use his newfound powers to recoup his losses. This was especially acute for offices bought in the provincial administration (Haldon, 2005: 30-37).

In 535, laws were passed against corruption, and in addition to prohibiting the selling of offices, Justinian set the "custom" at a fixed rate. Officials could not have a criminal record, and bribery was relentlessly pursued. An important practical measure to prevent corruption was to increase the salaries of officials, but even at the end of his reign, Justinian continued to grapple with corruption.

In 536, Justinian forged laws to reform the administrative structure of the empire. This reform affected provinces across Eastern Europe, and it essentially enhanced administrative districts while creating stronger territorial units. This was done by subjecting multiple provinces to the power of one ruler. For example, the provinces of Pontus, Elenopont, Polemonsky, Macedonia and Dardania, Paphlagonia and Gonoriada were consolidated, and in Egypt, one ruler governed two provinces of Libya.

Naturally, this also had important military effects in each region as well. (Johnston, 1999: 120-128). Justinian spoke frankly about the reasons for their necessity, primarily the manner in which they strengthened the power of the governors to deal with frequent uprisings among the indigenous tribes inhabiting the empire. The government's desire to destroy the separatist tendencies of the provincial nobility was equally as significant as the desire to stop all rivalry between the civilian and military authorities at all levels. (Johnston, 1999: 130-132).

Chapter 6: Justinian's Financial Policy

An ancient coin depicting Justinian

The Achilles heel for Justinian's reign was his financial policy, because once in power, Justinian wanted to impress his subjects with his generosity and charity. In the tradition of old Rome, he gave the people luxurious games, especially horse racing, since bloody gladiatorial games had been banned by Constantine the Great. He gave large sums from the treasury for the reconstruction of the eastern provinces of cities affected by earthquakes and other natural disasters, and across the country, he built charitable institutions such as hospitals, nursing homes and hotels. Of course, no reform is possible without transportation, so he restored roads, bridges, aqueducts, and the city's cisterns.

Ancient bust of Constantine

Soon, the need for money forced Justinian to bury any higher tax rates and, in contrast, focus all his energy and attention on the search for new resources. War, construction, diplomacy, bribery for barbarians and luxury items depleted state coffers even in the wealthiest of cities, and in the process of trying to restore New Rome to the old, Byzantium was led to the brink of financial disaster. The way out of this situation was the strengthening of the means of tax collection and finding new ways of extracting money from the wealthy.

Financial reform came in the form of the talented a financier and administrator, John the Cappadocian, who put in charge Praetorian prefecture. Originally from Caesarea in Cappadocia, John was a man of low origin who was initially uneducated, rude, superstitious and vicious, but with his repulsive manners, he was able to confront the arrogant wealthy and, to the cheers of the peasants, use his official imperial position to extract the cash that had been illegally wrested from the peasants in the first place (Rosen, 2007: 120-124).

However, John the Cappadocian was distinguished by his greatest feature: originality. Even Procopius, who hated John, was forced to admit his statesmanship, political sagacity, tireless energy and the ability to overcome difficulties in this most miserable job. Coming from the people, there was no question that extracting more from the moneyed classes was an added bonus for him. The wealthy were the only targets because they actually dealt with currency rather than in-kind payments, he needed to clip the wings of his most virulent opposition, and because they had money. It made no sense to tax peasants who made up the backbone of the state and the army, largely because they did not work in currency and had little to give. (Haldon, 2005: 49-55).

Furthermore, Justinian realized that a strong, loyal and contented peasant population was essential to basic justice and the well-being of the empire, Alexander Vasiliev summarized his mentality: "Justinian saw and understood the defects of the administration expressed in the venality, theft, and extortions which caused so much poverty and ruin, and which inevitably aroused internal troubles. He realized that such a state of things within the Empire had evil effects upon social security, city finance, and agricultural conditions, and that financial disorder introduced general confusion into the life of the Empire. He was truly anxious to remedy the existing situation. He conceived it to be the emperor's duty to introduce new and great reforms, which he viewed as an obligation of imperial service and an act of gratitude to God, who bestowed upon the emperor all his favors." (Vasiliev, 1958: 159).

The program of financial reforms undertaken by John had the effect of making Justinian popular with the peasants while harming the nobles, and he also sought to centralize the financial administration to make it more flexible and less corrupt. The point was to keep taxes public rather than private, and to do this, he had to limit the arbitrariness of the nobility. In medieval societies, it was the local, grasping nobles that spurred rebellion, so controlling the elite was identical to curbing corruption.

The lack of money in the treasury pushed John the Cappadocian further in finding ever new ways to extract resources, to the point that an attempt was made to increase revenue from the domains of the emperor. Imperial estates in the 6th century grew rapidly, partly due to confiscations of the land of political opponents and any vacated land, and they were scattered throughout the empire, particularly in Egypt, Syria, Palestine, and Asia Minor. In order to increase their profitability, Justinian introduced the most high-tech forms of irrigation known at the time in 531, so the crown estates became model farms (Haldon, 2005: 39-44). Moreover, in terms of administration, Justinian refused to make a distinction between his personal property and that of the state. He subordinated the domains of the emperor, empress and the royal house to curators attached to the administration, so curators essentially became the servants of the imperial couple, meaning that all land was public, including Justinian's wealth and that of his family.

An important way to generate additional revenue under Justinian was to raise various indirect taxes and extraordinary payments, including trade monopolies, which had been used in Rome but had been canceled at one point. The grant of a trading monopoly came with a fixed price for goods sold (within the maximum imposed by the government), but the lack of competition came with the state's fee, which was huge. This generated tremendous revenue without granting the lucky company any relief from state oversight.

In other cases, often in Italian cities, Justinian waived taxation and granted a limited monopoly on pricing at their discretion. In exchange for these privileges, the government demanded payment from traders making up for the lack of investment in things had there been competition. The introduction of monopolies gave a wide scope for the abuse of government power, but Justinian's administrative reforms and pay increases made this less likely.

On top of this, the finance ministers came up with other methods of making money. In 528, the marine police became customs officers. Formerly, they inspected ships and prohibited certain goods, but now, they became revenue collectors for all goods disembarking cargo ships. Even the entrance to the capital harbor was taxed (Haldon, 2005: 44-49). John the Cappadocian also forced the repayment of arrears and all interest. It was easier to collect from powerful magnates since they did not want a long court battle with the state, they had money, and they could probably pay but had chosen not to. One element that might be considered an error was Justinian's refusal to abate taxes or forgive debts. This was an old Roman idea, but only in eras of tight central authority. Justinian, given his mission, could not afford this obligatory show of mercy.

Justinian provided free services to Constantinople's ordinary citizens on a very large scale. Emperor Anastasius in his time strictly limited and regulated the conduct of this distribution, but Justinian increased it as a means to counteract his high taxes and prices. First of all, he forced grain producing areas to sell at low prices for the sake of feeding the city poor. Justinian, often at his own expense, traveled throughout the empire searching for the lowest cost for grain and would buy the quantities needed. Since cheap bread was bought by higher taxes, Justinian's use of his own money to buy grain bargains undoubtedly impressed his subjects.

Another less impressive tax revenue source was the obligation for members of a commune to pay tax on abandoned land. Whether the land was planted or not, those living adjacent to it, even if they did not have the manpower to farm it, were still responsible for it. Another way to view this is to say that there was a single tax levied on land communes. If the community goes from 100 to 75 members, the tax remains the same. Neighbors with abandoned plots (such as those of soldiers killed in war) were assigned these and taxed for them. On the one hand, this was a sign of generosity and could, in theory expand peasant holdings, but it was also a tax on land that many did not have the resources to exploit.

John F. Haldon summarizes and appraises Justinian I and his financial reform: "In reviewing Justinian's reforms and interventions in the administration of the empire, therefore, it is possible to see his program as dictated largely by his own ideological priorities, but with a strongly pragmatic and, to a certain extent, philanthropic element. The tensions between the welfare of his subjects, the efficient running of the state's fiscal and judicial machinery, and the vested interests of the metropolitan and regional social elites of the empire determined the effectiveness of his measures." (Haldon, 53). Of course, these sorts of problems have always tormented governments.

Chapter 7: Justinian's Ecclesiastical Policy

Ancient coins that depicts Justinian wielding a cross

Although Justinian himself was a very competent theologian and is now even considered a saint in the Eastern Orthodox churches, he never questioned the principle that questions of the faith must come from the synod. The essence of Justinian's view of the church is summarized in the concept of "symphony:" it was an anachronism to speak of "church and state." Byzantines would never make such a distinction in the sense of a realm of "secular" politics where the faith had no place.

For Justinian, the question was not "between Church and State" but rather between two different social structures with the same origin and purpose but with different methods. The reality of the symphony sets both the crown and the body of the faithful (which is much more accurate than "church and state") in mutual cooperation, mutual support and mutual responsibility, without the intrusion of one body at the expense of the other. The church was the true law of daily life. Family law, moral issues and even weights and measures were legislated in the synod, and this synod, generally speaking, was elected.

In Justinian's *Novellae*, for example, bishops had to be monks of high moral standing. Bishops who had a worldly career needed to spend 15 years as a humble monk before any consecration to bishop. The church itself was guaranteed its independence by the inviolability of her property, the populist strength of the monasteries, and their own independent court system.

The Novella 132 legislated certain punitive measures against heretics. Some of this might make modern people uncomfortable, but no more so than the modern ability of powerful individuals to break their social inferiors with long lawsuits and expensive legal representation. Heretics, regardless of one's opinion on the theological issues involved, were a threat to the state. Novella 45 also states that religious classes could not hold civil service posts. The rationale was that those at odds with the state should not be in the defense forces of that state. A heretic, whatever else he was, was an opponent of the Orthodox emperor. Furthermore, there were as many heretical emperors as Orthodox ones, so the discrimination had a tendency to go in circles, especially in the early empire.

Monophysitism was the main heresy of the era. Earlier, Arianism had that distinction, but, though still extant, it was not the threat it had been under Constantine. The Monophysite heresy stated the following: the human aspect of Jesus is combined with His divinity. This creates a new person, a single individual, the God-man. The Orthodox party argued that the human nature (and all things pertaining to mankind, including culture and government) need to be separate from divinity, or things of the spirit. This means that the two natures form a single person, but each has its sphere in the life of Christ, the church, Christian government and everything that is both created and rational (Gray, 215-220).

The Monophysite view was held by a majority of the population in Egypt and the East, so it could not simply be solved by force. Still, Justinian combated heresy throughout his life, and his chief assistant in the cause was his wife Theodora, who performed a role similar to the modern concept of "minister of religion."

It would be an error to believe that the Monophysite heresy was purely academic. It went to the heart of human behavior. When concerned with the persecution of heretics, the issue was not abstract doctrine but behavior. Pope Leo wrote, "In what way could [Christ] really accomplish the truth of his mediation unless he who in the form of God is equal to the Father were also a sharer of ours in the form of a slave: so that through one new man there might be a renewal of the old, and the bond of death contracted by the transgression of one man might be released by the death of the one man who alone owed nothing to death? For the pouring out of the blood of the righteous on behalf of the unrighteous was so powerful in its claim, so rich a ransom that, if the whole community of captors believed in their Redeemer, tyrannical bonds would hold no one." (Wessel, 2008: 252). Leo the Great, one of the more articulate defenders of the Orthodox position, was arguing that justice is impossible if the natures of Christ combine to create a new creature.

Pope Leo the Great

The Fourth Ecumenical Synod was that of Chalcedon, and its effects were epochal. Justinian and his predecessors had tried to conciliate both parties with vague phrasing, but this satisfied no one. These compromises were vehemently condemned by the pope of Rome and yet again, communication between religious leadership in the east and west was severed. Eventually, papal legates brought to Constantinople a decree to be signed by all the Eastern bishops and the emperor himself. It stated that the Roman See had never deviated from the Orthodox faith. It was less controversial to sign Leo's statement on the matter of Chalcedon, but Rome's specific role was rejected.

Justinian was at least the second emperor to deal with this claim, but for him, union with Old Rome was of paramount importance. Thus, it would be a mistake to assume that both parties suddenly came to an identical understanding of how power and authority in the Church was wielded. The Greeks agreed that the church of Old Rome was the bulwark of the faith on this most divisive issue, and Justinian continued to attach enormous political significance of the Roman bishop in virtue of his vision of Roman unity.

The reconquest of the Western empire also necessitated a very different approach to the papacy. Without the cooperation of Rome, the Byzantine Empire would be that much less legitimate. Justinian's position over the heresy was to support the moderates over the extremists, but Rome would have none of it. At the time, the pope in Rome was Agapetus. Justinian, eager to please him, installed a moderate in Constantinople named Anthemius. Agapetus objected on the grounds that he already was a bishop and should not switch Sees. Later, Agapetus discovered some moderate Monophysite ideas, and then his resolve stiffened. At the same time, Justinian's military forces in South Italy had been bogged down in a war of attrition, meaning that Agapetus could have his way. He personally deposed Anthemius and imposed his own hierarch, but when Agapetus died a short time later, Justinian had more freedom to impose Orthodox bishops throughout the empire. (Saris, 2006: 205-208).

Chapter 8: Justinian's Foreign Policy

Replica of a coin depicting the reconquest of Africa

In its foreign policy in the west, Justinian was guided above all by the idea of the restoration of the Roman Empire, but to implement this ambitious plan Justinian had to subjugate the barbarian states that emerged from the ruins of the Western Roman Empire. The first to fall were the Vandals in 534. The Vandals had created a fleeting state in North Africa, but the restoration of the Roman slave system and the new taxes in the conquered provinces caused protest. Byzantine soldiers also became angry that the government did not provide them some of the conquered land for themselves. In 536, units in North Africa under Constantinople rebelled and joined local Barbary tribes and runaway slaves. Only in the mid-6th century did North Africa finally submit to the authority of the empire (Saris, 2006: 1-7).

Another victory was the conquest over the Ostrogothic state in Italy. After landing in Sicily during the summer of 535, Belisarius quickly captured the island, crossed into southern Italy, and began the successful drive north. With the help of the Greco-Italian slave-owning aristocracy and the Orthodox clergy, Belisarius captured Rome in 536. That the Goths and Vandals were Arians in theology was no small matter either given the empire's issues with heresy.

However, since Justinian's forces acted as conquerors, the arrogance led to a widespread popular movement under Totila the Ostrogoth in 551-552. Totila was a talented military leader and visionary politician. As a representative of the Ostrogothic nobility, he was not willing to abolish slavery, but at the same time, he needed popular support against the far superior infantry of the Byzantines. Totila took into his army a group of escaped slaves and serfs and gave them freedom, and he also began to support free land tenure and private property in the Ostrogothic world. He even began to confiscate the estates of large Roman proprietors, especially those deemed to be sympathetic to the Byzantine empire. This provided him with the support of all sectors of the Italian population suffering from Justinian's imperial policy. Totila took Rome in 546 and soon conquered Greek-speaking Italy, Sicily, Sardinia and Corsica (Rosen, 2007: 137ff).

A medieval depiction of Totila

At the same time, Totila needed to be concerned with his rivals in the Ostrogothic nobility. Many noble Ostrogoths began to see their popular leader as too strong. Often, Totila made concessions to the Ostrogothic and Italian nobility, thereby alienating them from the masses and causing them to lose supporters. In 552, Byzantium counter-attacked with a huge army commanded by Belisarius' successor, Narses, and in June of the same year, the battle of Tagin was lost by the Ostrogoths. Totila died in that battle, but resistance against the Byzantines remained consistent, and it was only in 555 that Italy was again part of a Roman empire (Rosen, 2007: 77-79).

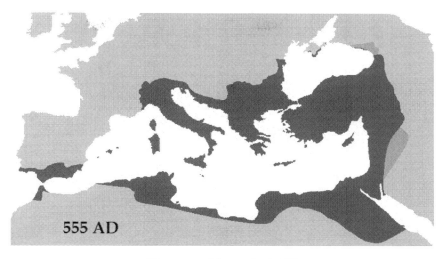

The extent of the empire in 555

As in North Africa, Justinian tried to preserve the slaveholding relation in Italy and restore the Roman system of government. In 554, he issued a "Pragmatic Sanction" canceling all of Totila's reforms, and land previously confiscated from the slaveowning aristocracy was restored. Serfs and slaves who had gained their freedom were again brought into subjection. At the same time, Justinian began a war with the Visigoths in Spain, where he was able to capture a number of strongholds in the south-eastern part of the Iberian Peninsula. At this point, it seemed that the dream of Justinian's restoration of the Roman Empire was within reach. The problem was that the Byzantine administration did not understand the political world that created Totila, and the dangerous practice of returning newly freed slaves to their masters ensured the empire enjoyed only a fragile dominance.

In the East, Byzantium waged a grueling war with Persia, her main rival overall. The most important goal of the Byzantine forces was the rich regions of Transcaucasia, especially the city of Lasik in modern-day western Georgia. Moreover, Byzantium and Persia competed in the silk trade (among other goods) from China, Ceylon and India. Using the fact that Byzantium was embroiled in a war with the Ostrogoths, the Sasanian king Khosrau attacked Syria in 540. Thus began a hard war with Persia which lasted intermittently until 562. Under the peace treaty, the city of Lasik was granted to Byzantium while Svaneti and other areas of Georgia were given to Persia. Byzantium was required to pay an annual tribute to Persia, but this was to offset the losses incurred by being banned from the coast of the Mediterranean and Black Seas.

In addition to that fighting, war also erupted in the northern parts of the empire, most notably the Balkans. Avars, Huns, Bulgars, Heruli, Gepids and other barbarian tribes and peoples crossed the Danube and attacked the northern cities of Byzantium. Especially dangerous to Byzantium were invading Slavs. The last years of Justinian's reign were marred by a terrible invasion of Slavic hordes that devastated Thrace and came to the very walls of Constantinople. In such circumstances, the emperor once again turned to Belisarius, who for several years had retired in peace and was almost forgotten. Belisarius needed few troops to defend the capital, and he successfully repelled the barbarians. Signs of love and gratitude were extended to him by the people when returning to the capital, which, unfortunately, aroused displeasure in a suspicious Justinian. Soon, the emperor unearthed a conspiracy against him. One of the suspects, under torture, said that he was acting on secret orders from Belisarius. That was enough to deprive the honored commander of honor, property and freedom. A few months later, he was acquitted.

Justinian is sometimes accused of forgetting the economic development of the East. The east was the wealthiest part of the empire, the center of crafts and trade, and in his fervor for the west, he might have put fewer resources into the proper hands for the development of this heartland of the empire. It is possible that the fragility of Justinian's success stemmed from this, but it's also unlikely that these claims are true or fair. Byzantium was not in the business of spurring demand; the empire offered a highly stable currency and a fairly professional bureaucracy and court system. Italian states slaughtered each other for the privilege of trade concessions with the emperor. Justinian however, given his grandiose plans, did maintain strong economic ties in the west. The diplomatic activities of the Byzantine government were close to the commercial interests of the country.

In the 6th century, Byzantine diplomacy brought together both merchants and Christian missionaries in search of new trade routes penetrating deep into the African continent, in Asia, the Caucasus, and the Crimea. Constantinople at the time was the center of world trade and controlled the exchange of goods between Europe and Asia, and the largest economic centers of the empire were Alexandria, Antioch, Edessa, Ephesus, Smyrna, Nicaea and Nicomedia in Asia Minor. In addition, Tyre, and Beirut were also being reconstituted as trade hubs. For the European part of the Byzantine Empire, the four major cities were Thessalonica, Corinth, Patras, and Thebes, but the wealthiest cities of the empire were all in the east.

The Byzantine Empire under Justinian led a lively trade with many countries and peoples. A primary role in the economic life of Byzantium at this time was trade with the major eastern cities. From Byzantium, as before, the exports included handicrafts, the finest linen and woolen fabrics of Asia Minor, Syria and Egypt, as well as amazing works of jewelry, glassware, leather goods, iron, grain, wine, drugs, and papyrus. In exchange for these goods, Byzantine merchants (mostly Egyptian and Jewish) traded for raw silk, ivory, precious stones, pearls, pepper and spices, incense, ebony, dyes, and slaves. (Rosen, 2007: 296-298).

Simultaneously, the Byzantine government vigorously sought to establish overland trade links with China through their outposts in the Crimea, the Bosporus, Kherson, and Caucasus. As a result, Byzantine merchants built trade relations with the steppe nomads who lived north of the Euxine Pontus. Increased trade with the peoples of the Black Sea region and the Caucasus fed the empire with exports of furs, wax, honey, leather, and livestock. They imported goods such as luxury goods, textiles, iron, grain, oil, salt, salted fish.

Byzantium eventually built its own silk industry, which at the time was a state secret of the Chinese. According to legend, two Nestorian monks took two silkworm eggs and hid them in their hollow staffs. Silk-weaving workshops in Antioch, Tyre, Beirut soon gained immense profit. Large public workshops for the production of silk fabrics were established under Justinian in Constantinople itself. Understanding the importance of silk, the Byzantine government introduced a state monopoly on it, and soon the imperial silk-weaving workshops had become one of the main sources of income for the urban administration.

Somewhat less important in the economic life of Byzantium in the 6th century was trade with the West. Byzantine merchants still operated in the barbarian kingdoms of Italy, Gaul, Spain and North Africa to trade in textiles, Syrian wine, silverware, papyrus, precious stones, spices, clothing, embroidery and glass products. Trading posts were erected or refurbished throughout Naples, Ravenna, southern Italy and Carthage, yet trade connections across the Mediterranean during this period was very difficult. Byzantine merchant ships in the Mediterranean were almost always threatened by Vandal warships, and Greek merchants in the barbarian kingdoms were sometimes persecuted and almost always resented.

Byzantine merchants, particularly the rich merchants of Constantinople, Antioch, Alexandria and other cities, were interested in the restoration of trade relations with the West. They advocated peace in the Mediterranean Sea and the extension of Roman power throughout the entire region. Not surprisingly, the aggressive plans of Justinian met with sympathy in these circles. However, these classes also had to pay for the military operations that would turn the Mediterranean into a Roman sea. Commercial interests in Byzantium generally supported Justinian. They needed the patronage of a strong central government, wide conquests in the West, and the military defense of the East.

Chapter 9: Justinian's Legal Reform

Justinian's military conflicts also spurred legal reform. To consistently fend off multiple attacks at once, the resources of the empire needed to be skillfully marshaled and command had to be centralized. Since these also drained the treasury, legal reform also influenced taxes, property and the income of citizens.

If anything, Justinian was primarily a great legislator. Law in the ancient mind was not a command restricting the freedom of humanity but an acknowledgment of the limitations of human nature and the affirmation of the purpose of the cosmos (Daube, 1969). Freedom was something achieved only after hard, ascetic labors that tamed people's passions. As a result, Justinian's Code and its derivatives reflected his dream of a new Roman empire that could conquer and hold the west and Africa.

Justinian's Code consisted of four elements. The *Institutes* presented a systematic exposition of the foundations of all law, the general principles of law enforcement and a systematic exposition of the axiological principles of private law. These were divided into 4 books and 98 titles under the headings: 1) a general theory of law and the doctrine of the rights of subjects; 2-3) common institutions of property law and personal security; and 4) the doctrine of the claims and the principles of law in court procedure (Watson, 1998).

Among the most fundamental concepts of legal culture in the Institutes is that of justice, itself coming from *jus*, the term for law. Justice was to render to each his due. The knowledge of this legal idea is the systematic understanding of divine things, human needs and the essential attributes of just and unjust ideas. Technically, a law cannot be unjust, since then it is not a law. It becomes a "decree" or "command," terms considered more neutral (Daube, 1969).

The *Digests* were the bulk of the corpus. They were meant to be a systematic compilation of the works of the most famous Roman jurists, such as Ulpian or Julian. In total, the *Digest* consists of excerpts from thousands of Roman documents. It was a kind of encyclopedia of Roman jurisprudence, but it also reflected contemporary legislative priorities. (Crook, 1984: 10-21).

The *Codex* was the systematization 4600 imperial laws, making up 12 books and 765 titles. Church law, public service, legal procedure, and legal precedent were molded into a detailed system of law striving to be both consistent and connected with the past. Here, past emperors, Senators, ancient customs, and the tradition of the early Republic were brought together as a systemic whole. (Daube, 1979).

The *Novellae* are the fourth part of Justinian Code and deal primarily with the writings of previous emperors. Using modern terminology, they are a compendium of executive orders.

Taken together, the legal code was a monstrous, profound and colossally significant codification of Roman jurisprudence, history, legal thought, religion and philosophy. To carry out the codification, Justinian issued a decree on February 13, 528 creating a special committee of ten experienced lawyers headed by eminent jurist Tribonian. The Commission carefully examined the contents of the three previously mentioned codes, and by the following year, 12 volumes had been approved. The confusion of conflicting laws, decrees and traditions had been taken a long way towards coherence.

One of the programmatic statements of the *Institutes* reads, "Civil law is thus distinguished from the law of nations. Every community governed by laws and customs uses partly its own law, partly laws common to all mankind. The law which a people makes for its own government belongs exclusively to that state and is called the civil law, as being the law of the particular state. But the law which natural reason appoints for all mankind obtains equally among all nations, because all nations make use of it. The people of Rome, then, are governed partly by their own laws, and partly by the laws which are common to all mankind. We will take notice of this distinction as occasion may arise." (Watson, *Institutes* of Justinian, Bk 1, sec 2-1).

Justinian's new code truncated the use of the death penalty. Punishment was not to harm the offender but to restore the authority of the law. It was a means of re-balancing the crime with the victorious imposition of the natural law itself. The law binds the ruler as a Christian, and it permitted saints such as Ambrose or Theodore the Studite to openly challenge emperors who had overextended their power (MacMullen, 1997: 12-18) The emperor used the law to eliminate church corruption, especially in the purchase of the office of bishop. To the Byzantines, Christianity did not render the Roman law void but only revealed the true origin of law in general. Being responsible to God was something taken seriously at the time, and this weighed on the emperor (Evans, 1996: 60-63). In a strong sense, punishment was a means of righting an imbalance that unnatural acts introduce into the world.

Justinian also acknowledged in his legal code that the law is binding on him as a man and as a Christian. The only time he could modify its usage or change the law in any way was in the interests of righteousness (Evans, 1996: 192). For example, while the law on paper might command that all debts to the state are to be paid, Justinian and many other emperors violated the letter of the law to forgive debts for the lower classes.

In terms of canon law, Justinian was active in these areas as well. One novella was addressed in 535 to the patriarch of Constantinople. It discusses a number of matters, such as the marital status of the clergy, church property, the residence of bishops, obstacles to ordination, the legal status of the clergy, religious education, and many other areas. The canonical rules of Justinian became the standard of the Roman and Greek churches and remain so to this very day. In the introduction to this novella, Justinian made his famous statement: "The greatest gifts of God, showing his supreme benevolence are the priesthood and crown: sacred and imperial power."

Legally, despite some tradition pointing to the hereditary transfer of power, there was never a valid legal scheme for succession. The Byzantine system of government was focused primarily with the problem of ensuring the integrity of a extensive multinational empire itself within a multinational state. In principle, any ethnic group could occupy the highest positions in the state, including the status of emperor. As a result, even though the empire was quite international, nothing stood in the way of unity, and the Byzantine sense of justice was based on the understanding of the law as the general will of the population (Pound, 1906: 70-77).

The status of a person was not derived from the privileges of a particular social group but belonged to him by virtue of citizenship. The rule of law here meant the formal equality of all citizens regardless of their social, ethnic, economic, or ethnic origin. Since Byzantium believed itself to be the legal center of the world, multilingualism was a critical feature. The presence of these factors helped create a doctrine of formal rights as part of the Institutes (Johnston, 1999: 69-74).

Each person had a certain legal status in Roman law, but during one's life this was not necessarily permanent. However, the basic provisions governing the personal and the political status of each citizen were inviolable. These include the right to life, education, marital status, the right to bequeath and inherit, the right to participate in a variety of contracts, and the right to judicial protection and procedural status. The code is not normally interpreted as a body of rights, but it is clearly seen even in a quick reading of some key provisions. Even the Emperor did not have immunity from judicial prosecution.

Conclusion

The Byzantine idea was strictly universalist. Throughout the empire's long history, the Emperor was considered the incarnation of law. The church is established directly by God, but the state is required for its discipline, regularity and protection, so emperor and church exist for the common good. Thus, the concept of the "church" being subordinated to the "state" is both a neologism and a misnomer, so to the Byzantines, the emperor was a religious institution. While the civil service, army and urban administration might have some relation to the modern idea of "state," the Emperor does not, since he was not essentially a political figure.

The concept of "divine right" did not develop until the modern age, so to apply it to either Otto or Justinian is anachronistic. Their authority was from God in the same sense that natural laws are. The emperor was an element of God's law on earth, but with a specific and limited set of powers. His role was to identify and eliminate the effects of free will. Human beings without law are like the body without a brain (Ullmann, 1964: 93-94).

The term "absolute rule" is also an anachronism. Even if Byzantine theory established that there was nothing the emperor could not do, the realities of technology, communication and decentralization made such action impossible. The large civil service, the army, the monastics, the bishops, cities and merchants all placed both de facto and de jure limits on royal power. Justinian admitted in his new law code his own submission to law. The only time he could suspend its application or alter the law itself was in the interest of justice (Evans, 1996: 192-202). For example, while the law might state that debts are to be paid if legally incurred, Justinian could abrogate this law to protect poor peasants against their lords. One aspect of the increase in civil power and legal regularity was to create an emperor powerful enough to fight the rich and powerful without becoming so powerful as to be overbearing. While this is a tall order for any society, Justinian and some of his successors came fairly close.

As such, in the process of reestablishing and reforming Roman power, perhaps Justinian's greatest legacy was his internal policy, especially in his codification of older Roman laws adapted to the new realities of the Christian era. In 528, precisely in his identification as Roman emperor, Justinian established a commission to revitalize and reform the law code. Ultimately, after many years, the *Corpus Juris Civilis* was published and included the laws, a digest and summary of the laws, and the Institutes, forming a guide for students of essential legal principles (Evans, 2005: 175-176).

In fact, the concept of Roman emperor was so essential for Justinian that all acts of his reign were based on its essential assumptions. His attempt to unite the western parts of the empire that had fallen to the barbarians was an attempt to make his claim as sole world ruler a reality. To be clear "world ruler" only meant one thing: that since there is one God, there is also one law and one church. This implies that there can only be one government, albeit made up of different states and nations (Wickham, 2005: 175-176).

Although he's still famous today, it's necessary to remember the failures of Justinian's reform. Justinian's ambitions required high taxes, great military expenditures (especially since his reconquest of the west was not successful) and increased centralization, which (to the emperor) were all in the interests of justice. Justinian's high standards meant that, quite often, fallible human beings would not reach it.

Bibliography

Sarris, Peter (2006) Economy and Society in the Age of Justinian. Cambridge University Press

Brown, Peter (1989). The World of Late Antiquity. W.W. Norton

Bryce, J. (1914) The Holy Roman Empire. Macmillan

Johnston, David (1999) Roman Law in Context. Cambridge University Press

Nicholas, Barry (1969). An Introduction to Roman Law. Oxford University Press

Stein, Peter (1999). Roman Law in European History Cambridge University Press

Watson, Alan, ed (1998). The Digest of Justinian, Revised English-language Edition. University of Pennsylvania Press (Two volumes)

Buckland, WW (1939). A Manual of Roman Private Law. Cambridge University Press

Buckland, WW (1975). A Textbook of Roman Law from Augustus to Justinian. Cambridge University Press

Pound, Roscoe (1906) Readings in Roman Law. Jacob, North and Company

Crook, John (1984) Law and Life of Rome. Cornell University Press

Daube, David (1979). Forms of Roman Legislation. Clarendon

Daube, David (1969) Roman Law: Linguistic, Social, and Philosophical Aspects. Edinburgh University Press

Johnston, David (1998). Roman Law in Context. Cambridge University Press

Jolowicz, Herbert F. and Barry Nicholas (1972). Historical Introduction to the Study of Roman Law. Cambridge University Press

Jones, Arnold and Hugh Martin (1968). Studies in Roman Government and Law. Praeger.

Cameron, Averil (2000) The Cambridge Ancient History, Vol. 14. Cambridge University Press

Cumberland, Torsten (2009). The Gothic War. Westholme

Evans, JAS (2005). The Emperor Justinian and the Byzantine Empire. Greenwood Press

Evans, JAS (1996) The Age of Justinian: The Circumstances of Imperial Power. Routledge

Maas, Michael (ed. 2005). The Cambridge Companion to the Age of Justinian. Cambridge University Press

Gray, John (2005) The Legacy of Chalcedon: Christological Problems and their Significance. In Mass (ed) The Cambridge Companion to the Age of Justinian. Cambridge University Press, 215-238

Pazdernik, J (2005) Justiniaic Ideology and the Power of the Past. In Mass (ed) The Cambridge Companion to the Age of Justinian. Cambridge University Press, 185-215

Haldon, John F (2005) Economy and Administration: How did the Empire Work? In Mass (ed) The Cambridge Companion to the Age of Justinian. Cambridge University Press, 28-60

Rosen, William (2007). Justinian's Flea: Plague, Empire, and the Birth of Europe. Viking

MacMullen, R (1997). Christianity and Paganism from the Fourth to Eighth Century. Yale University Press

Wickham, C (2009). The Inheritance of Rome: Illuminating the Dark Ages 400-1000. Penguin

Vasiliev, AA (1958) History of the Byzantine Empire, 324–1453. University of Wisconsin Press

Sirks, AJB (2008) The Colonate in Justinian's Reign. The Journal of Roman Studies, 98: 120-143

Hudson, M (2000) How Interest Rates Were Set, 2500 BC-1000 AD. Journal of the Economic and Social History of the Orient, 43(2): 132-161

Ullmann, W (1964) Reflections on the Medieval Empire. Transactions of the Royal Historical Society, 14: 89-108

Ierodiakonou, K (2002) Byzantine Philosophy and its Ancient Sources. Oxford University Press

Made in the USA
Columbia, SC
23 January 2023

10896270R00026